Vladimir

ARCHITECTURAL
LANDMARKS

Aurora Art Publishers·Leningrad

On *the foretitle*:
  Symbol of the city of Vladimir
On *the title-page*:
  Vladimir.
  Panoramic view of the city

Introductory essays
by NIKOLAI VORONIN
Selection and notes on the plates
by STANISLAV MASLENITSYN
Photographs
by VALERY BARNEV,
VLADIMIR MONIN and
ALEXANDER STREBKOV
Designed
by VLADIMIR SMOLKOV
Translated from the Russian
by ALEXANDER SOKOLOV

© Aurora Art Publishers, Leningrad, 1988
Printed and bound in the USSR

B $\dfrac{4902020000\text{-}667}{023(01)\text{-}88}$ 5-88

ISBN 5-7300-0168-1

One of the oldest Russian cities, Vladimir lies in exceptionally beautiful surroundings on the high left bank of the river Kliazma. The site cut through by deep ravines is an elongated triangle whose apex points to the east. It is formed by the valley of the river Lybed (now flowing inside a culvert) in the north and the Kliazma in the south. Way across the Kliazma in the south there extends its water-meadow fringed by the blue-green line of woods receding to the horizon. The terrain further rises north and east across the valleys of the Lybed and the Irpen. Nestling comfortably on the rolling hills are the villages of Dobroye and Krasnoye which are now almost part of the city. Both can be seen from a long distance for their prominently sited churches. In ancient times the town was bounded by pine woods on the western side.

Archaeologists have found evidence of a Finno-Ugric settlement that existed on the high table-land in the south-east at the beginning of the Christian Era. Later, in the tenth and eleventh centuries, the place attracted members of Slavonic tribes, the Krivichi and Slovenes from the Smolensk and Novgorod lands respectively. The lasting attraction of the site rising forty to fifty metres above the Kliazma was due to the natural protection that it offered because of its difficult access.

The Kliazma, a big and mighty river at the time, was meandering across the wide water-meadow at the foot of Vladimir Hill on its way to join the Oka thus linking the land between the two rivers with the Volga, the old trading route of Eastern Europe. It is for good reason then that later, in the twelfth century, one of the gates of Vladimir, that opening onto the Kliazma, was named the Volga Gate. The area on the outskirts of the Kievan state, which was known as the Zalessky Krai, the land "behind the forest", and where the towns of Rostov and Suzdal had already existed, abounded in natural wealth. Its forests teemed with furred animals and its rivers and lakes with fish. The water-meadows of the rivers were ideal for raising cattle, but the main attraction of the site was the vast and fertile treeless plain north-east of the Kliazma.

It was only natural for the Kievan princes, therefore, to have turned their gaze early to the rich and populous North-Eastern Rus. In the eleventh century it became a possession of Prince Vsevolod Yaroslavovich (1030—1093) and his descendants. At the end of the eleventh century a bloody internecine struggle broke out over the possession of North-Eastern Rus. In the course of the feudal war it became obvious that the high ridge above the Kliazma, overlooking the hostile Riazan and Murom Principalities, was of decisive defensive importance and protected Suzdal on the south-east. This fact led to the transformation of the peaceful settlement of traders and artisans into a formidable fortress. Natural contours determined the exact size and shape of the fortress built in 1108 by Prince Vsevolod's son, Vladimir Monomakh (1053—1125). The fortress was protected by the precipitous bank of the Kliazma in the south and the steep slopes of the Lybed river valley in the north; in the west and east there were deep ravines linked up by artificial moats at their tops. Without doubt, the newly built fortress had gate towers through which passed the road between Kiev and Suzdal. The fortress was enclosed on all sides with huge ramparts topped by wooden walls.

The first stone church, a Church of the Saviour, was built by Monomakh somewhere within the walls of the fortress, most probably at the high point of the town above the Kliazma. The new town was named Vladimir after its founder. The irregular quadrangle of the fortress became the nucleus of the future capital city of North-Eastern Rus.

Vladimir Monomakh's successor, Prince Yuri Dolgoruky (1090—1157), was too absorbed with his struggles for the Kievan throne to pay much attention to his northern possession. Shortly before his death, however, apparently seeing the futility of the struggle in the south, he launched a far-reaching construction campaign of more city-fortresses in the Suzdal land, among them, Moscow. In Vladimir, he built a new Prince's Court with a white-stone church consecrated to St. George, the patron saint of the princes (1157). The Court was sited on the elevation at the edge of the southern slopes of the hill, west of Monomakh's fortress. By the mid-twelfth century the town grew extensively towards the east along the road to Suzdal. Among the inhabitants of Vladimir were people who had come from towns of the Dnieper area, including Kiev, torn by internecine strife. Hence the Kievan names given to the local rivers: the Lybed, Irpen and Pochaina. The river valleys had retained until the last century such old names as Prince's Meadows and Yarilo's Valley, the latter being a hangover from the pagan past.

The fast-growing young town, populous, rich and strategically located, was destined to become the capital of the Vladimir Principality. Yuri Dolgoruky's son, Prince Andrei Bogoliubsky (ca. 1111—1174), transferred the throne of the grand prince to Vladimir, then a city of artisans and traders. The townsfolk rallied around the princes of Vladimir in the struggle against the old autocratic boyar families. They were also the main force behind the drive to increase the political superiority of the Vladimir lands launching a courageous campaign to unite the country rent by chaos and feudal division. The years 1158—65 mark a period of fervent, large-scale building in the city. Belts of new ramparts were built circling its unprotected sections west and east of Monomakh's fortress, which was to become the Middle Town. As was the case under Monomakh, the western border of the new fortress was formed by the ravines winding their way down towards the Kliazma and the Lybed. The Volga Gate, located at the foot of the Middle Town and leading to landing stages on the Kliazma, as well as the Irininy and Mednyie Gates opening onto the ravines leading down to the Lybed, were built of wood. The so-called Golden Gate of white stone stood on the city's longitudinal axis — the road to the south. At their tops, near the fortress, the ravines were linked up by a deep moat spanned by a bridge at the Golden Gate. South of the gate there are still remains of the western Kozlov Val (rampart). Built next to the Golden Gate and Prince Yuri's Court was the Court of Prince Andrei Bogoliubsky with the white-stone Church of the Saviour. The city's western side was obviously the part where princes and boyars lived. The sloping eastern wedge-shaped part of Vladimir formed a posad, trade and artisan quarters. The posad was also protected by ramparts and walls. Built of white stone on its eastern side was the Silver Gate at the bridge across the Lybed and along the road towards Prince Bogoliubsky's residence and Suzdal (remnants of the rampart, the so-called Zachatyevsky Val, can be seen today behind the houses on the northern side of Frunze Street). The Middle Town was referred to in the later chronicles as "Pecherny" (cave), the western side as the "Novy" (new) town, and the eastern side was later called "Vetchany" (decrepit) because its fortifications, neglected over the centuries that followed, became decrepit and crumbling for lack of maintenance. The total length of the walls and the ramparts in Vladimir by that time exceeded seven kilometres, more than those of Kiev and Novgorod.

Built in the high south-eastern part of the Middle Town was the major Cathedral of the Assumption (1158—60). Together with the white-stone chapels of St. George and the Saviour, also located on the southern edge of the city, the Cathedral of the Assumption formed the most striking architectural ensemble in the city's south. Its longitudinal axis was formed by these gate towers: the Golden Gate, the Trade Rows Gate (in the western wall of the Middle Town), the Ivanovskiye Gate (in the eastern wall) and the Silver Gate in the eastern end of the triangle-shaped city.

The next stage in the architectural history of the city came in the late twelfth and early thirteenth centuries. The consolidation of power of Grand Prince Vsevolod III nicknamed the Big Nest (1154—1212) and the growth of political awareness of the townsfolk resulted in serious uprisings. The Prince's Court was moved to the southern part of the Middle Town to flank the Bishop's Court. A sumptuous stone palace was erected there together with the Cathedral of St. Demetrius (1194—97). A stone wall with defensive gates was erected around the residences of the Prince and the Bishop (1194—96) as protection from the rebellious townsfolk. Badly damaged in the 1185 fire, the Cathedral of the Assumption had new walls built, which increased its size and stressed the importance of the citadel as the architectural centre of the city. Founded in the Middle Town's south-eastern corner was the Prince's Monastery of the Nativity with a white-stone church (1192—95) to form as it were a second internal fortress. The city's busy market place was moved to the northern part of the Middle Town (across 3rd International Street) looked over by the formidable walls of the citadel. There in 1219 Vsevolod's successor, Prince Constantine, built a small Church of the Ascension. The wife of Vsevolod III, Princess Maria, established the Convent of the Assumption (the Princess' Convent) with a cathedral built of brick (1200—1) in the north-eastern corner of the New Town.

Thus, over the years the city of Vladimir and its architectural ensemble were taking shape. The most important feature of this ensemble, structures of white stone, were not numerous because at that time most of the churches were built of wood. There is evidence that a wooden church of St. Nicholas stood in the twelfth century on the sloping bank of the river behind the Golden Gate, with wooden structures of the Ascension Monastery perched on the high ridge next to the church. Obviously, houses of townsmen by that time extended beyond the confines of the New Town. An account in the chronicles of the big fire that occurred in Vladimir in 1185 mentions thirty-three churches having burnt in it. Apparently, the fire caused great damage to numerous dwellings as well — ordinary townsfolk and even wealthy merchants and boyars lived in wooden houses.

In the twelfth and thirteenth centuries the three sections of the city fitted into the triangle formed by the courses of the Kliazma and the Lybed. Running through the whole city was the main street with four gate towers (it ran along the present-day Moskovskaya, 3rd International and Frunze streets). People entering the city through the Golden Gate could see on the right side the courts of princes with the churches of the Saviour and of St. George, and on the left, at a distance, the structures of the Princess' Convent. The buildings were set against the background of the blue vastness of the Kliazma water-meadow and the woods stretching away behind it. The space straight ahead was bordered by the rampart and the wall of the Middle Town with the wooden tower of the Trade Rows Gate. Looming beyond the wall in the city's corner was the massive five-domed Cathedral of the Assumption.

The Middle Town formed the city's centre. On its right, seen beyond the citadel's white-stone wall, were the gold-domed Cathedral of the Assumption, the bishop's court, the structures of Vsevolod's Palace (1154—1212) set on the flanks of the Cathedral of St. Demetrius, with the cathedral of the Monastery of the Nativity behind them. On the left there was the market place and the Church of the Exaltation of the Cross beyond which fields stretched away to the horizon. Right in front on the slope of the plateau of the Middle Town there lay the eastern belt of its walls forming the base for the Ivanovskiye Gate surmounted by a tower. Outside this wall began the posad, or trading and artisan quarters of the city, where all the houses and churches were of wood. At this point the city's triangle narrowed down, and the built-up area resembled a big village stretching along the road. This impression was enhanced by the vastness of the open spaces seen from there in the south and the east. The main street ran through the white-stone arch of the Silver Gate to merge with the road leading to the villages of Dobroye and Bogoliubovo, and to Suzdal. It is unknown exactly where the cross-streets originally intersected with the main one. The small width of the posad suggests that opening onto the main street were many short by-lanes (as is the case today). Considerable area in the Middle Town was taken up by the Market Place upon which converged roads originating in the north-eastern part of the territory. In the New Town there apparently was a lateral street running along the ramparts of the Middle Town in the ravine and on towards the Volga Gate on the Kliazma and the Medniye Gate in the north on the Lybed. There was perhaps a street running to the north-west from the Trade Rows Gate towards the Irininy Gate.

Various groups of picturesquely arranged buildings unfolded before the observer not only inside the city. But perhaps the most important aspect of the city's architecture was its breathtaking façades, clearly designed to be admired at a distance. In achieving this, the builders of Vladimir made skilful use of the rich landscape of the high river bank.

The city could be seen from the Yuryev road as if from overhead and all the variety of its architecture could be viewed as a whole. By contrast, the view from the hills down which the road from Suzdal ran in the east caused the city to appear to be leisurely sprawling over the elevating terrain. Straight ahead was the Silver Gate with a cluster of townsfolk's homes and tall wooden churches. Rising at some distance behind them were the walls of the Middle Town with the Ivanovskiye Gate and towers. Still farther, on the left, there shined the domes of the Monastery of the Nativity and of the citadel.

But undoubtedly the finest view of the city could be obtained from the riverside, taking in the wide water-meadows and forests, through which meandered the road to Murom. From the river the city was seen in all of its majestic splendour reminiscent of the panorama of Kiev on the high bank of the Dnieper. Perched on the hill in the west were the wooden structures of the Monastery of the Ascension and the Church of St. Nicholas. Extending down the slope from the southern corner of the New Town was the wall which then ran along the ravine and again climbed the steep hill at the Volga Gate towards the corner of the Middle Town. Set on the slopes of the semi-circular depression beyond the wall, the homes of the townsfolk were barely visible, buried in thick patches of green. On the high ridge above them could be seen princely courts with the churches of the Saviour and of St. George and high-pitched roofs of palaces. Visible at the corner of the Middle Town were the soaring domes of the Cathedral of the Assumption — the major landmark in the panorama. Set on the same line with it and at nearly equal intervals were smaller cathedrals, those of St. Demetrius and of the Nativity. Erected at the edge of the flat-land, they created the illusion that the entire city was built up with similar white-stone structures. The city's skyline gently and rhythmically descended from the Cathedral of the Assumption, its highest point.

The skyline of the Vetchany part of the city, the *posad*, dominated by the tops of wooden churches and the tent-shaped roofs of towers, was more fragmented.

Undoubtedly the fine architectural array of the city, far from being a matter of luck or chance, was preconceived by its builders. The somewhat "ostentatious" quality of the architectural monuments of Vladimir built during the times of Andrei and Vsevolod III is characteristic of the city as a whole.

The second half of the twelfth century saw the flowering of culture in Vladimir Rus. It resulted from the progressive policy of Vladimir princes who, together with townsfolk and the gentry, rallied against the efforts of feudal lords to fragment the country. This policy promoted a signal development of architecture and art and gave rise to lively literary ferment. Local chroniclers of those times praised the staunchness and patriotism of the people of Vladimir. To further enhance the power and glory of the Vladimir land, the chroniclers described numerous miracles associated with the famous icon of the Virgin of Vladimir. Originating in the same period was a tale about the slaying by the boyars of Prince Andrei Bogoliubsky. It is remarkable for its sense of tragedy and superb style. All the surviving works reflect a high level of artistic achievement rooted in the traditions of Kievan literature and folklore. They are imbued with the single political idea of the right of Vladimir to rule over a united Russian land. But unfortunately the forces clamouring for disintegration gained the upper hand, and with the death of Vsevolod III, the unity of the Vladimir land was also at an end. These events made inevitable the terrible peril that was brewing in the steppes.

In 1238, the hordes of Mongol-Tartars attacked Vladimir. After a persistent siege the city was taken, pillaged and burned. But even after this disaster, the city continued to be regarded as the centre of North-Eastern Rus and the guardian of its political and cultural traditions. In the late thirteenth and early fourteenth centuries it was the seat of the Metropolitan of All Rus. It was in Vladimir's Cathedral of the Assumption that the coronation of the Great Prince took place. Meanwhile "The Great Principality of Vladimir" was the subject of contention between the dynasties of Moscow and Tver, who were trying to emulate Vladimir's fine architecture. Dmitry Donskoi took over the patronage of the Cathedral of St. Demetrius which contained the ancient icon of St. Demetrius of Thessalonici and the most precious icon of the Virgin of Vladimir. The former was transferred to Moscow in 1380 shortly before the Battle of the Kulikovo Field; the latter was temporarily moved to the Cathedral of the Assumption in Moscow. Thus Moscow inherited Vladimir's historical traditions and received for safekeeping its twelfth-century relics as well. In 1408, following the devastating raid on Vladimir by the hordes of Khan Yedyghei, in which the Cathedral of the Assumption burnt, Prince Vasily I sent to Vladimir Andrei Rublev, an artist of genius associated with the revival of Russia, to restore the cathedral's painting. In 1410, the city suffered another devastation at the hands of the horde of Khan Talych. In 1469, a famous Moscow builder, Vasily Yermolin, restored the damaged Golden Gate and the Church of the Exaltation of the Cross at the Trade Rows. However, Vladimir's fortifications were never restored to their former dimensions. In 1486 only the wooden walls of the Middle Town were rebuilt and then further renovated in 1491 and 1536. The walls of the western and the eastern third of the city gradually came to ruin. At the turn of the fifteenth century, builders from Moscow reconstructed the Cathedral of the Assumption in the Princess' Convent.

From that period onwards Vladimir became a minor city of Muscovy, a city of a glorious past and venerated relics, growing at an extremely slow rate. In 1489, the deportees from Novgorod formed their own settlement called Varvarka across the Lybed. The mid-sixteenth century saw the formation across the Lybed of two more settlements called Streletskaya and Pushkarskaya which later merged to become the Streletskaya settlement. Formed in the seventeenth century were the settlements of Nizhny Borovki and Verkhny Borovki. Legend has it that the latter also became home for displaced people of Novgorod and that the large brickwork house of the Babushkin family of merchants was supposed to have been built in the sixteenth century. The city's population at that time was small. For example, the settlements of Pushkarskaya and Streletskaya had twenty households all in all in 1584 while in 1592 there lived a hundred of *streltsy* (hereditary soldiers). In those years, right outside the Golden Gate there was the Yamskaya Sloboda, a settlement of imperial coachmen with their own wooden Church of Our Lady of Kazan. Outside the settlement there was a pine-tree forest. In 1668, the city's total population numbered 990 and there were 400 houses. Artisans lived in its eastern section and traders in the western. In 1684, in the Market Place there was the Gostiny Dvor (a trade arcade) housing 392 small shops and the Church of St. Parasceva, the patron of trade.

The building of stone structures was resumed in the seventeenth century. They, of course, cannot be compared with the "golden age" of Vladimir architecture, but builders of those times saw to it that the style of their structures did not clash with the city's old architecture. In 1649, for example, the merchants of Vladimir built in the posad the exquisite Church of the Nativity of the Virgin which blended perfectly with the city's southern panorama. The white-stone gate of the citadel was used as the basis for putting up the enormous tent-shaped bell-tower which added a vertical sweep to the ancient architectural centre of Vladimir. Another such bell-tower, but more ornate, was built in the Monastery of the Nativity alongside the Holy Gate adorned with painting. Early in the eighteenth century the old wooden fencing was replaced by a stone wall which formed something like a decorative "kremlin" in the south-eastern corner of the Middle Town. The small Church of St. Nicholas was built near the Church of the Saviour in the old Prince's Court as well as a plain-looking, square bell-tower aimed to enhance the imposing appearance of the group of twelfth-century structures. This trend to enrich the city's southern "façade" was continued by builders in the eighteenth century, when stone churches — the Church of St. Nicholas-at-Galeya outside the Kozlov Val (1715) and the Church of the Ascension (1724) — were erected on the sites of the old wooden ones.

A sketch map of Vladimir drawn up by an icon painter in 1715 gives some idea of what the city looked like by that time. Its centre was formed by the kremlin with wooden walls and towers built between 1491 and 1536 on the old earthen ramparts of the Middle Town. Eight of the eighteen towers faced south. This was due to the builders' considerate attitude to the city's southern "façade" rather than a military stratagem. Right there, on the slope of the hill, they planted the so-called Patriarch's Orchard. The square north of the cathedral was a densely built-up area with a rather conspicuous house of the voivode (a military leader). North of Bolshaya Street there were densely populated areas with twisting alleys, and right beside the middle Tainitskaya Tower in the north the old pond was still preserved, which had been used to store water in case of another siege. Closer to the eastern Trade Rows Gate there was a prison fenced off by paling. The city's western side was given over to trading and the main street in the north widened to form a market place filled with rows of stalls and workshops. Bolshaya Street was the only one in the city paved over with oak planks. The other streets were reminiscent of muddy country roads. There was a village-type settlement outside the Golden Gate. The same haphazard pattern was characteristic of the part of the city across the Lybed and of its eastern part where as little as 1,840 people lived by the start of the eighteenth century.

The old monuments of the city sustained great damage in the eighteenth century. The wooden fortress was pulled down, which started an uncontrolled razing of the earthen ramparts. The white-stone churches of the Saviour and of St. George, burnt out in the 1778 fire, were torn down and new ones were built instead. The top of the Golden Gate was rebuilt. In 1778, Vladimir was made the centre of *namestnichestvo*, an administrative district, and in 1796, of a province. The new plans for redesigning the old city, unlike many other perfunctory plans calling for "regular" layouts for Russian cities, showed some discretion as regards its ancient landmarks. The plans provided for preserving what had been left of the twelfth-century ramparts and the old long street running across the whole city. The local architects corrected some of the worst errors made by the St. Petersburg compilers of the plans. For example, they prevented the construction of two buildings of the Gostiny Dvor (Trading Arcade) in the open space fronting the Cathedral of the Assumption and the Cathedral of St. Demetrius. The structures would have blocked the view of the cathedrals from Bolshaya Street. And yet, they built the enormous Office Building (1785) between the cathedrals, whose monotonous barrack-like mass spoiled the beauty of the city's southern "façade". In general, the development of the centre of the provincial capital was based on the city's old layout. Built on the eastern edge of the central area was the Governor's House (1808). The northern edge of the square was formed by two buildings in the style of Russian classicism: the Noblemen's Club (1826) and adjoining it the Gymnasium for Boys, refashioned from the merchant Petrovsky's house (1840). The tallest feature of the city's skyline became the bell-tower of the Cathedral of the Assumption built in 1810 instead of the former tent-roofed one destroyed by lightning.

A whole block on the northern side of Bolshaya Street was occupied by the Trading Arcade (1787—90) which separated from the main street in the Market Place, and part of which can still be seen at the corner of Lenin Street. Farther towards the Golden Gate protruded the portico of the Church of St. Nicholas at the Golden Gate (the church has not survived) whose colonnade matched those of the buildings of the central square. Finally, the Golden Gate, standing on the street's axis, was flanked with round corner towers.

The industrial development of Russia that followed did not make any significant impact on Vladimir, which remained a small city of traders, artisans and clerks. The city fathers did not treasure Vladimir's beauty and its old monuments. The city mayor, merchant Nikitin, for instance, proposed a barbarous project to convert the Golden Gate into a water tower. They did not dare to carry out this project but instead built a new tower on the Kozlov Val, an eyesore in one of the city's most scenic spots. The city's main street came to be built up with tenement houses and shops, whose backyards faced the picturesque southern slope of the city covered with a jumble of small homes of fairly well-off citizens. The section of the railway between Moscow and Nizhny Novgorod was built at the foot of the slope which disfigured the beautiful southern panorama of the city.

Today, the precious historical monuments of Vladimir and the region belong to the Soviet people. Even during the difficult years of the Civil War ways and means were found to maintain these monuments in good repair. One of the first projects undertaken by Soviet scholars and researchers was to clean the twelfth- to fifteenth-century frescoes in the Cathedral of the Assumption. Since that time the attention of researchers to the outstanding artistic and architectural monuments for which the Vladimir land is famous has been constantly growing. The city now is the centre of a vast region with well-developed industries and farming; it is an important cultural centre of the Russian Federation. Vladimir has been included into the Golden Ring international tourist route.

Nikolai Voronin

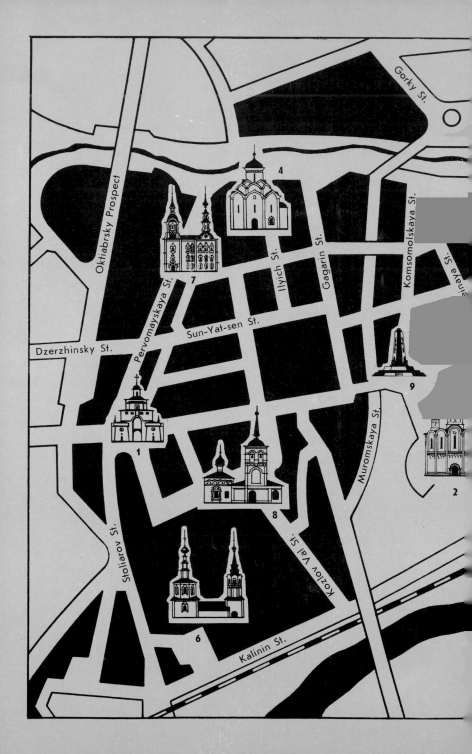

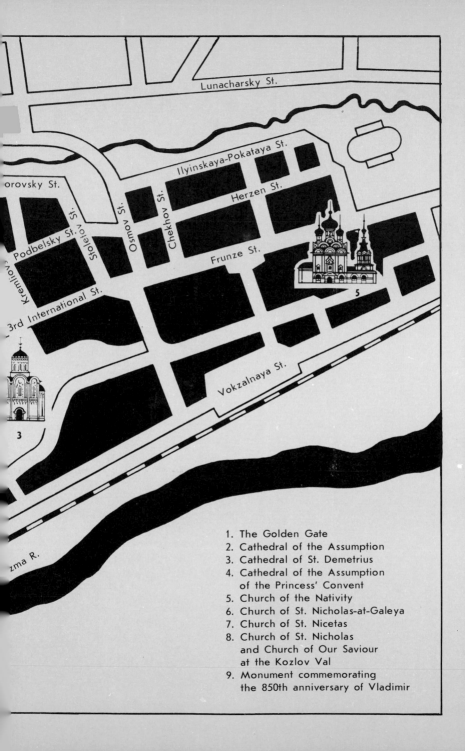

Lunacharsky St.

Ilyinskaya-Pokataya St.

orovsky St.

Herzen St.

Podbelsky St. St.

Stoletov St.

Osmov St.

Chekhov St.

Frunze St.

Kremljov's

3rd International St.

5

Vokzalnaya St.

3

zma R.

1. The Golden Gate
2. Cathedral of the Assumption
3. Cathedral of St. Demetrius
4. Cathedral of the Assumption
   of the Princess' Convent
5. Church of the Nativity
6. Church of St. Nicholas-at-Galeya
7. Church of St. Nicetas
8. Church of St. Nicholas
   and Church of Our Saviour
   at the Kozlov Val
9. Monument commemorating
   the 850th anniversary of Vladimir

Vladimir

1. Vladimir. View from across the Kliazma

The Cathedral of the Assumption is still the dominant part of the city's skyline. Standing on the steep left bank of the river, the cathedral is visible from a great distance to anyone coming from Murom or Riazan. Its shining central dome can be seen from a distance of ten to twelve kilometres. In the twelfth to seventeenth centuries the stone structures of the cathedrals and the churches towered above the city walls behind which were hidden the dwellings made mainly of wood. The impression was that the city consisted entirely of majestic stone structures spread over the high bank.

2. Symbol of the city of Vladimir (see also the image on the foretitle)

A lion rampant, historians believe, was the personal emblem of Prince Andrei Bogoliubsky, the first ruler of Vladimir-Suzdal Rus in the middle of the twelfth century. In 1673 a lion rampant with a long-staffed four-pointed cross held in its front paws became the city's official symbol. The symbol is listed among the crests of Russian cities in the reference book compiled by order of Tsar Alexei Mikhailovich and splendidly illustrated by artists of the Armoury. In the eighteenth and nineteenth centuries, the lion with the cross was always included in the symbols of all towns in Vladimir Province.

2

3

3. Monument in honour of the 850th anniversary of Vladimir. 1958

The obelisk designed by A. Dushkin was unveiled in 1958 in Ploshchad Svobody (Freedom Square). The sculptured figures of a Worker, Soldier and Architect set at its sides are by D. Riabichev. Architect A. Dushkin

4. A 1715 map of Vladimir

The map was drawn by an icon painter rather than by a cartographer, but it gives a fairly true picture of the city in the early eighteenth century. It can be gathered from the map that Vladimir's central part in those years was encircled by high log walls and towers built on the ridge of the ancient ramparts over the period of 1491—1536. The map shows the Patriarch's Orchard on a patch of land sloping down towards the Kliazma. The many towers along the southern wall were meant not so much for defence as to lend the city an impressive and beautiful look from the Kliazma, a navigable river at that time.

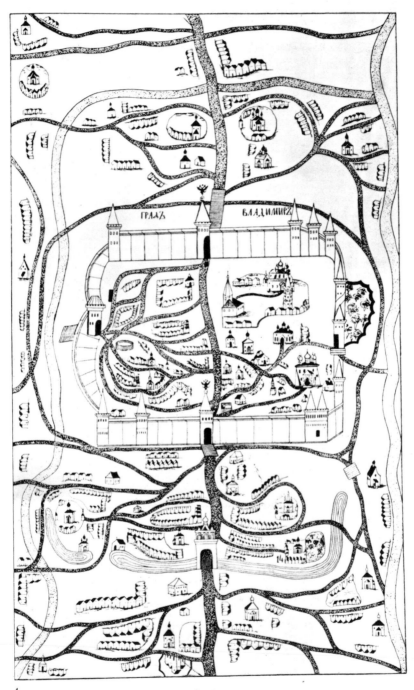

5

5. Cathedral of the Assumption. 1158—89; 19th century. View from the north-eastern side

Prince Andrei Bogoliubsky contributed to the upkeep of the city's main cathedral vast tracts of land and a tithe, in the tradition of the great princes of Kiev, who contributed a tenth of their revenues to the upkeep of the city cathedral. Erected in 1158 by Andrei Bogoliubsky's builders, the cathedral was the tallest in Rus in the middle of the twelfth century. It was built of white stone and its exterior decorations included reliefs, colourful frescoes and gilding. According to ancient chronicles, Andrei invited "craftsmen from all parts of the earth" to build the cathedral, and among them were craftsmen, who, it is said, were sent to Rus by Emperor Frederick Barbarossa.

6. Cathedral of the Assumption. 1158—89. Western façade

As they enlarged the cathedral in 1158, Vsevolod III's craftsmen marked off on the cathedral's western façade the limits of the former three-nave building. According to chroniclers, Prince Vsevolod III employed no foreign builders or architects in reconstructing the cathedral. The 1185—89 building became a model for cathedrals in the centuries to come. For example, in 1470 it was pointed out to the Italian architect Aristoteles Fiorovanti as a model for the construction of the Cathedral of the Assumption inside the Kremlin in Moscow.

23

7. Cathedral of the Assumption. 1158—89. View of the domes from the bell-tower

The central golden dome survives from the original building. The drum of the dome is pierced by twelve tall windows. During the restoration of the roofing over the vaults in the late nineteenth century the semi-circular upper sections of the outer walls of 1158 were exposed, as they were somewhat higher than the vaults of 1189. The domes of the cathedral look especially majestic against the background of the river meadow and the distant forests.

8

8. Cathedral of the Assumption. 1158—89; 19th century. View of the bell-tower from the north-western side of the city square

The cathedral was badly damaged in the 1185 fire in the reign of Prince Vsevolod III. During the repair work it was greatly enlarged: new walls were built around the three old ones, the old apses were replaced by new ones, and four new domes were added on the cathedral's corners. The cathedral became twice as large, and up to four thousand people could gather inside it. Over the ages it went through repeated repairs and additions. In 1810, a bell-tower was built next to it. Systematic restoration of the former appearance of the remarkable twelfth-century monument was undertaken between 1882 and 1891. The first restoration efforts at the end of the nineteenth century were supervised by the noted Russian historian and archaeologist Ivan Zabelin. The cathedral was freed from the later additions, its original helmet-shaped domes and the semi-circular upper sections of

the walls were uncovered. It was at that time that the first frescoes of 1160—89 and 1408 were found. Wide-scale scientific restoration work started in the cathedral in 1918 continues to this day.

9. Lion mask corbel in the western gallery of the Cathedral of the Assumption. 1186—91

This ferocious lion was supposed to keep evil spirits away from the cathedral and to instill fear in ordinary folks.

10. Female mask corbel in the western gallery of the Cathedral of the Assumption. 1186—91

The remarkably expressive female masks on the cathedral's walls were perhaps symbols of virtues.

11

11. Female mask. Relief on the southern façade of the Cathedral of the Assumption. 1158

Masks of this type were usually placed on the central parts of façades. Like lion masks, they personified the forces of kindness and protected the buildings against evil spirits. This relief, like the preceeding one, was transferred from the 1158 building onto the one built in 1185—89.

12, 13. Lion masks. Reliefs on the northern façade of the Cathedral of the Assumption. 1158

Lion reliefs were the most widespread forms of sculptured decoration in Ancient Rus. They were put on the façades and the internal walls of churches in Vladimir in the twelfth and thirteenth centuries. People of those times thought that images of lions placed on the sides of the cathedral's entrances or windows kept evil spirits at bay. The lions also represented the princely power and were reminders that the shrines had been built thanks to the prince's generosity.

14. Young Hebrew. The central figure in the composition Three Young Hebrews. Relief on the Cathedral of the Assumption. 1158

The cathedral built by Andrei Bogoliubsky had quite a lot of sculptured images. Some of them were transferred onto the façades of the reconstructed building. The composition Three Young Hebrews was dismantled in 1185—89 and mounted inside a zakomara on the new northern façade. Prince Vsevolod's builders did not always show reverence for their predecessors' handiwork. They sometimes placed the reliefs at random or even used them as building material.

12   13

14

15

15. Cathedral of the Assumption. 1158—60. Northern façade

In 1918—20 the restorers discovered remains of the 1158—60 frescoes on the northern wall of the original building. The band of blind arcading on the façade of the 1158 cathedral had wider intervals between the arches. Some of the arches had narrow apertures in them to let in more light. The blind spaces of the arcading had painted images of prophets holding white scrolls. Painted above the window niches of the arcading were blue peacocks and bands of floral patterns on the sides of the windows. The band's columns were gilded. The richly decorated band of arcading looked striking on the white stones of the structure. As time went on, the architects of the Vladimir land started to use reliefs instead of painted patterns inside the arches of bands of blind arcading and on the façades of churches.

16. Icon: *The Virgin of Vladimir.* First half of the 12th century
Tempera on wood. The Tretyakov Gallery, Moscow

Leaving Vyshegrad (near Kiev) Prince Andrei took along this remarkable icon painted by an outstanding Byzantine painter. Legend has it that Andrei transferred the capital to Vladimir because the icon "directed" him to do so. The icon became a religious and political palladium of the prince and of the Vladimir Principality. The prince took the icon along on his military campaigns. Already during Andrei Bogoliubsky's lifetime the icon became the most sacred thing in the Cathedral of the Assumption in Vladimir and a symbol of the power of the Vladimir-Suzdal and then Moscow grand princes. In 1480 the icon was taken to Moscow to the cathedral of the same name. In 1918 several layers of overpaintings were removed from the original image. As an outstanding work of art, the icon has been on display at the Tretyakov Gallery since 1930.

30

17

18

17. *St. Arthemius.* Fresco in the Cathedral of the Assumption. 1189

The Cathedral of the Assumption was given new internal painted decorations in the reign of Prince Vsevolod. The job was done by skilled artists who had a fine sense of proportion. Unfortunately, only insignificant fragments have come down to us of those interesting frescoes. The uncovering of what remains of the 1189 frescoes under the layers of overpaintings had not yet been completed.

18. *An Angel and the Infant John the Baptist.* Fresco on the wall at the entrance to the altar in the Cathedral of the Assumption. 1408

Only the bottom part of the fresco survives. It depicts St. John the Baptist led by an angel through the desert. The desert is a rocky landscape with sparse dwarfish green trees. The image of the infant St. John is full of charm. Some researchers ascribe the fragment to Andrei Rublev, but stylistically it has more affinity with Daniil Chorny's 1408 frescoes. The figures of St. John the Precursor and the angel have dark contours painted around them; the projections of the hillocks are too graphic. The fresco lacks the softness and smoothness of line characteristic of Rublev's creations. The whole composition is artistically perfect but a bit dry.

33

19. Cathedral of the Assumption. Interior frescoes. 1408

The princes of Moscow regarded the Cathedral of the Assumption in Vladi-mir as their shrine. For a long time Russian grand princes were crowned in this cathedral. In 1408, following yet another fire, the finest Moscow painters Andrei Rublev and Daniil Chorny were

asked to restore the cathedral's interior
painting. They in fact had to paint the
frescoes anew using the remains of old
ones to guide them as they went about
their job.

20

←

20. *St. Mark, St. John and Angels.* Detail of *The Last Judgement* fresco in the Cathedral of the Assumption. 1408.
A copy by N. Gusev
The A. Rublev Museum of Old Russian Art, Moscow

The Last Judgement murals in the twelfth-century churches of Vladimir-Suzdal Rus were usually painted on the vaults and walls beneath choir-galleries where princes and their retainers attended the service. The figures of the apostles and angels were placed in the centre of this large-scale composition right above the crowds of worshippers.

←

21. *St. Matthew, St. Luke and Angels.* Detail of *The Last Judgement* fresco in the Cathedral of the Assumption. 1408.
A copy by N. Gusev
The A. Rublev Museum of Old Russian Art, Moscow

The worshippers could see the faces of their future judges during the service and, perhaps, tried to fathom the expression on their faces and to find in them answers to their innermost thoughts.

23

22. *St. John.* Detail of *The Last Judgement* fresco in the Cathedral of the Assumption. 1408

Andrei Rublev and Daniil Chorny lent each of the characters in the mural features that they thought conveyed man's spiritual perfection. The apostles' faces exude kindness and compassion and for this reason the images created by the painters seem beautiful and perceivable to every spectator.

23. *St. Luke.* Detail of *The Last Judgement* fresco in the Cathedral of the Assumption. 1408

Whilst Andrei Rublev and Daniil Chorny regarded kindness and sympathy as the foremost qualities of man's spiritual beauty, the faces of the apostles are strictly individual and at the same time each conforms to the canons of the icon-painting tradition.

24

24. *Angel.* Detail of *The Last Judgement* fresco in the Cathedral of the Assumption. 1408

People who gathered inside the cathedral must have felt special warmth and kindness in the faces of the angels depicted standing in rows behind the judging apostles. The angels' faces expressed every degree of compassion for people's destinies. They were look-ing at the worshippers with an expression of mild anxiety as they softly bent their heads of fluffy hair. The figures of the angels already convey the measure of perfect harmony which was to guide Andrei Rublev at the time he was creating his masterpiece *The Old Testament Trinity*, an icon for the Trinity-St. Sergius Monastery as a tribute to its founder St. Sergius of Radonezh.

25. *Christ in Majesty.* Detail of *The Last Judgement* fresco in the Cathedral of the Assumption. 1408. A copy by N. Gusev

The A. Rublev Museum of Old Russian Art, Moscow

The image of Christ on the vault of the middle nave is the centre of the big composition. Christ "coming to judge the living and the dead" does not appear to the viewer a threatening and implacable ruler of people's destinies. On the contrary, his soaring figure surrounded by angels is filled with kindness and sympathy to people. The artist depicted Christ as looking affably at humanity and prepared to be not so much a judge of their deeds as a trusty confessor and cordial lord of the "kingdom of the righteous".

26. *St. Peter Leading the True Believers.* Detail of *The Ascension of the True Believers into Heaven* fresco in the Cathedral of the Assumption. 1408

The image of St. Peter is one of the most inspired creations of artists who did the decorative painting inside the Cathedral of the Assumption early in the fifteenth century. His image has been made so definite, looking so Russian that it can be called a portrait rather than a canonical image. This fact gives rise to controversy among researchers of old Russian painting as to whom to attribute the authorship of the image of St. Peter. Some think it is one of the undoubted works by Rublev in the Cathedral of the Assumption. But there are perhaps more grounds to suppose that the whole group of characters in *The Ascension of the True Believers into Heaven,* among whom St. Peter is

included, was done by one artist — Daniil Chorny.

27. *The Ascension of the True Believers into Heaven.* Detail of *The Last Judgement* fresco in the Cathedral of the Assumption. 1408. A copy by N. Gusev The A. Rublev Museum of Old Russian Art, Moscow

Old Russian painters usually endeavoured to subordinate their individual preferences to the interests of their joint ventures. But if viewed attentively, the whole set of frescoes nonetheless reveals some of the individual traits of each painter. In this scene, remarkable for the dynamism of its composition, the figures of the characters are shown to be in swift movement; their postures and gestures are impetuous. This composition is supposed to have been painted by Daniil Chorny.

28. *Jacob, Isaac and Abraham in Heaven*. Detail of *The Last Judgement* fresco in the Cathedral of the Assumption. 1408

This fresco also was obviously by Daniil Chorny. His manner of painting is distinguished by a degree of dependence on painting traditions of the fourteenth century. Daniil Chorny's drawing is daring and expressive but not quite correct. His human figures are a bit bulky and given too obvious contours.

→
29. *Abraham's Bosom*. Detail of the fresco in the Cathedral of the Assumption. 1408

Depicted against the background of the saint's robes is a group of children's heads. They symbolize the souls of children who, together with their forefathers, were fated to repose in Heaven.

→
30. *King David*. Fresco in the Cathedral of the Assumption. 1408

King David was widely revered in Vladimir-Suzdal Rus as early as the times of Andrei Bogoliubsky. His images in the sculptured decorations of churches of the twelfth century were always conspicuously set in the centre of the façades. King David epitomized a sage, powerful and just ruler elected by God's will. The king's image in the Cathedral of the Assumption of 1408 is attributed to Andrei Rublev.

31

31. Cathedral of St. Demetrius. 1194—97. View from the north-eastern side The court church of Vsevolod III was built at a period when his power was acclaimed as the greatest in the whole of Rus. The author of the famous epic *Lay of Igor's Host* said referring to Vsevolod: "... with your oars you can splash the Volga dry and drain the Don with your helmets", and that he could direct the actions of neighbouring princes the way an archer would direct the flight of his arrows. Devoted to Vsevolod's patron saint, the church on the premises of his court came to be the most sumptuous in Vladimir.

32. Cathedral of St. Demetrius. 1194—97. Apses

The top parts of the well-proportioned apses are decorated with blind arcading and deep-set window niches. The big windows let in much light to illuminate the altar part of the church.

33

33. Cathedral of St. Demetrius. 1194—97. Female mask corbel on the northern apse

Vladimir stone carvers favoured elongated female faces with large straight noses and eye sockets and widely separated eyebrows. Such masks were al-

ways distinguished by the softness of their lines.

34. Cathedral of St. Demetrius. 1194—97. Corbels of the central apse

A very amazing feature of the cathedral is the stone carving at the base of the

colonnettes of the blind arcading. Some
of the images, like the head of a bearded
man, attest to the fact that sculptors of
that period introduced some elements
of realism into their human masks which
they carved in accordance with the
church canon.

35. Cathedral of St. Demetrius. 1194—97. Western portal

The western portal of the cathedral has the most intricate and rich carving on the archivolt. Rising above the stepped niche of the main entrance of the cathedral, the archivolt covered all over with delicate carving resembles a *kokoshnik* (woman's headdress) made of most delicate lace.

36. Cathedral of St. Demetrius. 1194—97. Capitals of the colonnettes and stone carving of the western portal archivolt

The stone carvers covered the archivolt with representations of diverse beasts, birds, fantastic creatures and palmettes. The "stone lace" included griffins, birds and pairs of lions sharing a single head.

36

37. Cathedral of St. Demetrius. 1194—97. Decorations on the left section of the northern façade

At the top of the left section of the northern façade the carvers depicted Prince Vsevolod himself enthroned with his baby son on his knee, who was born while the cathedral was being built and named, as was the cathedral, after St. Demetrius of Thessaloniki. Vsevolod is surrounded by the rest of his sons bowing to their father. Such idealized sculptured portrayal of Vsevolod, the first in Vladimir-Suzdal Rus, was obviously intended to proclaim him as an equal among legendary Christian rulers. It is not by accident that his image on the cathedral's walls was placed on the same level as the image of King David.

38

38. Cathedral of St. Demetrius. 1194—97. Stone carving on the drum of the dome

The piers contain the images of Christ, prophets, evangelists, lions, griffins and birds.

39. *Princes Boris and Gleb and Arch-deacon Stefan.* Stone carving on the blind arcade of the northern wall of the Cathedral of St. Demetrius. 1194—97

The twelfth-century stone carvers of Vladimir were the first to place reliefs of saints inside the arches of blind arcading. Unfortunately, over the centuries a considerable part of these reliefs was replaced by new ones inferior to the original ones. Seven original carvings have survived on the northern wall. Most remarkable among these are the figures of the first Russian saints, Princes Boris and Gleb. In all, the cathedral's three walls contain in their arcature seventy images, only sixteen of which are old ones.

The twelfth-century reliefs of saints evince the consummate skills of their creators. The faces of the saints were intentionally carved in high relief while the other parts of each figure, which were perceived from a distance as a single whole, were done in low relief with masterful cuttings accentuating the folds of their robes.

40

40. Cathedral of St. Demetrius. 1194—97. Ornamentation of the central part of the northern façade

This was the first church in Vladimir to be so richly ornamented with white-stone carving. There is a total of 566 carved stones in the building's three walls not counting the carvings of the blind arcading. Only 46 images are symbols of the Christian religion while the rest are floral patterns, beasts, birds, griffins and other mythological creatures.

The narrow and tall niches of the windows have a series of receding arches inside them. It is a clever architectural trick which makes the windows look as part of the ornamentation rather than as simply deep slits in the walls.

41

42

43

41. *Human Dragon Fighting a Wild Beast.* Relief on the western façade of the Cathedral of St. Demetrius. 1194—97

Judging by his kindly and handsome face the man wearing a crownlike cap personifies goodness despite the fact that the lower part of his body is a dragon's tail. He is courageously fighting a wolf-beast. A noted Soviet historian, Academician Boris Rybakov, believes the character is the pagan god Simargl-Pereplut, who is sometimes identified with the sun-god Yarilo.

42. *Hercules and the Nemean Lion.* Relief on the western façade of the Cathedral of St. Demetrius. 1194—97

Medieval theologians maintained that Hercules' labours are on a par with those of the Biblical hero Samson who rent a lion.

43. *Griffin and Doe.* Relief on the northern façade of the Cathedral of St. Demetrius. 1194—97

The griffin, like many other mythical creatures, was borrowed from Eastern art. Medieval theologians thought of the griffin as of a "noble" creature and even believed that it was one of the symbols of Christ. In Byzantium and Rus the griffin came to be a symbol of supreme power and an emblem of valour and magnanimity.

44

45

44. *Two Lions with a Single Head.*
Relief on the northern façade of the
Cathedral of St. Demetrius. 1194—97

Such "heraldic" images of two beasts
with a single head, like a pattern where
birds have their necks intricately entwined, were quite frequent in the
twelfth and thirteenth centuries. They
were used not only in the decoration
of church walls but also in metalwork,
on fabrics for rich garments and in the
drawings placed on the margins of
books. The earliest records of such patterns are found in the countries of the
East. In Europe they began to be used
in the twelfth century. The Russian stone
carvers obviously wanted to amaze the
spectators with the unusual rather than
to instil fear in them.

45. *Birds with Entwined Necks.* Relief
on the western façade of the Cathedral
of St. Demetrius. 1194—97

The world of animal patterns carved on
the walls of the Cathedral of St. Demetrius is varied and fantastic. Researchers
are still trying to unravel the meaning
of many of the patterns. The monsters
are characteristic of the art of Eastern
countries but at the same time they can
be accounted for as borrowings from
bestial imagery of the Roman West. One
fact remains undoubted — each image
had a certain meaning well understood
by the people of the twelfth century.

46. *Wrestlers.* Relief on the southern
façade of the Cathedral of St. Demetrius. 1194—97

Creating the picture of a mythical world,
medieval stone carvers were always trying to be sure the images were readily
understood by all people. In executing
whole scenes and separate motifs they
could have been guided not only by
the special manuals containing ready
patterns but also by their own ideas
and experience. It is these images that
reflect the full measure of their ability
for realistic portrayal.

46

47. *Lion and Leopard.* Reliefs on the southern façade of the Cathedral of St. Demetrius. 1194—97

The mighty lion and leopard with palmettes on the tips of their tails are the beasts most frequently featured on the reliefs of Vladimir churches in the twelfth and thirteenth centuries. The medieval stone carvers showed remarkable imagination in depicting these mighty beasts of prey.

48. *Pheasants.* Relief on the northern façade of the Cathedral of St. Demetrius. 1194—97

This beautiful bird was a widespread decorative motif in medieval art. Russian masters could have borrowed the idea from the silverware of the Sassanid Empire and Byzantium. But the pheasants in the reliefs of the Cathedral of St. Demetrius have many very original features that set them apart from the known examples of portrayal of the birds in Oriental art.

49. *St. Theodore Stratelates.* Relief on the western façade of the Cathedral of St. Demetrius. 1194—97

Remarkable among the reliefs of the Cathedral of St. Demetrius are repre-

sentations of horsemen. They are saint warriors, patrons of princes on the battlefield. Some of them were the protectors of Vladimir princes, the successors of Prince Vsevolod. For example, St. Theodore Stratelates was believed to be the patron saint of Yaroslav Vsevolodovich, the father of Prince Alexander Nevsky, the famed military leader of the thirteenth century.

50. Cathedral of St. Demetrius. 1194—97. Interior. View of the princely gallery

From inside the cathedral looks bigger than it actually is. Tall and mighty pillars support the rather wide drum pierced by twelve tall windows. The light streaming through them on sunny days brightly illuminates the central part of the cathedral and particularly the special gallery built half way up the wall for the grand prince and his retinue.

51. *Lions.* Relief at the base of the arches in the Cathedral of St. Demetrius. 1194—97

Reliefs of lions were usually placed on the imposts in the princely churches of Vladimir in the twelfth century. They were a must but probably were not the only type of sculptured figures permitted in the interiors of cathedrals. Placed both on the interior and exterior walls, lions were symbols protecting the structures against the forces of evil and also indicated that the building belonged to the prince.

52. *Angel.* Detail of *The Apostles and Angels* fresco on the southern slope of the greater vault in the Cathedral of St. Demetrius. 1194—97

Experts say that the angels standing behind the apostles are painted in distinctly different styles. The difference consists both in the brushwork and in the types of faces depicted. Those painted on the southern vault have features typical of southern peoples: large dark eyes, small thin noses and sensual lips. They are painted in a poignant, fast and temperamental manner;

their dimensions are brought out with clear and fluid highlights.

53. *St. Andrew.* Detail of *The Apostles and Angels* fresco on the southern slope of the greater vault in the Cathedral of St. Demetrius. 1194—97

St. Andrew's face marked by wisdom can serve as a model of the beauty of old age. There are many excellent portrayals of old wise men in medieval art, but few painters of that time could rival this portrayal of St. Andrew remarkable for the amazing clarity in his gaze.

54. *The Apostles and Angels.* Fresco on the southern slope of the greater vault beneath the gallery in the Cathedral of St. Demetrius. 1194—97

Only insignificant fragments remain of the majestic composition *The Last Judgement* on the vaults and walls beneath the princely gallery. In 1918 they were discovered under the layers of over-paintings and became world-famous. The builder of the cathedral, Prince Vsevolod, was the son of a Byzantine princess of the Comnenus dynasty and he spent several years at the Emperor's court in Constantinople. He invited painters of the Constantinople school, the finest masters of monumental painting of the period, to paint the cathedral at his court.

55. *The Apostles and Angels.* Fresco on the northern slope of the greater vault beneath the gallery in the Cathedral of St. Demetrius. 1194—97

Sadly, many details of the splendid frescoes of the twelfth century in the Cathedral of St. Demetrius are lost. What remains of them still gives some idea both about the rather intriguing iconographic peculiarities of this remarkable cycle of paintings and its really noble and refined colour scheme. The colours that once were pale blue, lilac, greenish-yellow, dark purple, white and bright red added up to form an overwhelmingly grand spectacle.

→

56. *St. Paul.* Detail of *The Apostles and Angels* fresco on the northern slope of the greater vault in the Cathedral of St. Demetrius. 1194—97

The faces of the apostles are painted with striking perfection. Their features are very expressive and their characters are clearly distinct. This image of St. Paul, with a large forehead and a black beard touched with grey, ranks for its psychological characterization with the famous *St. Paul* by El Greco. By the side of the passionate and implacable St. Paul is the dreamy St. Matthew with a searching look. His delicate inspired face shows wisdom. The late twelfth-century master who did the fresco was a born colourist and a virtuoso painter. He made no preliminary drawings of the heads and painted with assured skilful strokes directly on the wet plaster.

55

←

57. *Angel.* Detail of *The Apostles and Angels* fresco on the northern slope of the greater vault in the Cathedral of St. Demetrius. 1194—97

The faces of the angels on the northern vault are different in structure from those on the southern vault. The faces are more rounded, their features are larger and more manly. They convey something typical of Slavic faces. The brushwork is less expressive but more eleborate. But at the same time these faces have many traits that hark back to the beautiful images of Greek art. More often than not researchers of St. Demetrius's frescoes are inclined to attribute the faces of the angels on the northern part of the greater vault to a Russian master who tried to emulate his precursor, an outstanding painter of the Constantinople school.

58. *St. Peter and the Righteous Wives.* Part of the fresco on the smaller vault beneath the gallery in the Cathedral of St. Demetrius. 1194—97

The painters most probably had in mind some specific personages when they depicted the righteous wives following St. Peter into Heaven. It is not by incident that two of them wear garments that mark them out as a Byzantine princess and a grand princess. Probably, one of them is the mother of the Grand Prince of Vladimir, a princess from the Byzantine Comnenus dynasty.

59. *Jacob, Isaac and Abraham in Heaven.* Fresco in the southern part of the smaller southern vault beneath the gallery in the Cathedral of St. Demetrius. 1194—97

The images of the forefathers who were granted the honour to be among the first to enter Heaven were most probably painted by a Russian master. They are painted diligently but with a perceivable degree of hesitation, uncertainty. In their day the frescoes on the southern vault under the princely gallery dazzled the viewer with their bright colours.

60. The Golden Gate. 1164 (with additions made in the 18th and 19th centuries). View from the western side

The white-stone gate built in 1164 completed the construction of the formidable ramparts around the city. The main gate to the city got its name from the Golden Gate of Constantinople and Kiev. Its oak doors were covered with sheets of gilded copper and it was topped by a golden-domed church dedicated to the Deposition of the Robe. During the long sieges of the city by the feuding princes, Tartars, Poles and Lithuanians, the Golden Gate stoop up well to the bombardments by stone missiles, the battering rams and fires. In 1469 the Church of the Deposition of the Robe was refurbished by Vasily Yermolin, a noted Moscow architect and sculptor. The church over the gate was rebuilt in 1687—91. In 1795 the architect Ivan Chistiakov started the construction of four round towers flanking the gateway and carried out more alterations in the church above the gate. The work proceeded very slowly and the new church was dedicated only in 1810.

61. Archway of the Golden Gate

What remains of the original gate are the two massive walls of big smooth blocks of white stone. The arch was even higher originally but over the time it has sunk nearly a metre and a half into the earth. Vladimir's Golden Gate was not only used to hold back the enemies but also to welcome Russian triumphant armies back from their campaigns. The ancient stones have witnessed many things. They remember Prince Alexander Nevsky, who lived in the thirteenth century and whose voice, according to an old chronicler, sounded "like a trumpet call among the people". The troops of Moscow Prince Dmitry Donskoi passed through the gate in 1380 after their victory over the Mongol-Tartars in the Battle on the Kulikovo Field. Early in the seventeenth century volunteers led by Prince Dmitry Pozharsky passed through it, as did in the eighteenth century the brave soldiers of the great Russian general Alexander Suvorov.

63

62. Vladimir. View of the old part of the city

The fancy tracery of the old streets of Vladimir covering the hilly bank of the river Kliazma looks picturesque at any time of the year. Only the churches with their tent-shaped bell-towers break up the otherwise monotonous line of squat wooden houses with stone floors which stand comfortably apart from each other here and there on the slopes.

63. Theatre Square in front of the city Drama Theatre near the Kozlov Val

64

64. Church of St. Nicholas (left) and Church of the Saviour at the Kozlov Val. 17th—18th centuries. View from the northern side

The small elegant Church of St. Nicholas has lavishly decorated platbands and rows of *kokoshniks*, the end faces of outer walls.

65

65. Church of St. Nicetas. 1762—65. View from the south-western side
This big three-tier church in baroque style was built with the money of the Vladimir merchant Semion Lazarev. Its walls are decorated with beautiful platbands and pilasters. Inside the building is divided into three separate churches each occupying one floor. The big windows let in plenty of light to illuminate their interiors and intricate gilded iconostases.

81

66. Ceramic tiles on the walls of the Church of St. Nicholas-at-Galeya. 1732—35

67. Church of St. Nicholas-at-Galeya. 1732—35. View from the north-western side

Chronicles of the twelfth century make mention of a church of this name. It stands at the foot of the hills where a landing platform used to be. The church with a tent-shaped bell-tower was built with the money of Ivan Pavlygin, a wealthy coachman of Vladimir.

67

68

69

68. The "slender candle" from the Church of Our Lady. 17th century
The Vladimir-Suzdal Museum-Preserve of History, Architecture and Art

The big hollow wax cylinders called "slender candles" were used for candlesticks put before the most revered icons. The decorative patterns were first traced on the surface, then the grooves were filled with soft coloured wax.

When the wax became solid, the entire surface was painstankingly polished.

69. The "slender candle". Detail

What looks like a decorative band is actually the names of merchants and city people who donated money to the building and decorating of the Church of Our Lady.

70. Church of Our Lady. 1649. View from the south-eastern side

Built with the money donated by the city merchants the church is typical of seventeenth-century stone churches built in trading and artisan quarters. Its tall central tetrahedral structure is topped off by two tiers of keel-shaped *kokoshniks*. The pediments of the tall drums of the five onion-shaped domes are also adorned by *kokoshniks*. The central structure of the church is organically surrounded on all sides by the numerous annexes in varying styles which enhance its massive size.

71. Cathedral of the Assumption of the Princess' Convent. Late 15th — early 16th centuries

The convent was founded by Princess Maria Shvarnovna, wife of Vsevolod III, who erected there a stone church in 1200 and 1201. Right from the time of its founding it was a court convent where princesses were also buried. The arcosolia built on the outer side of the cathedral contained in the thirteenth century the tombs of Maria Shvarnovna and her sister Anna, who was Vsevolod's second wife. The wife and daughter of Alexander Nevsky were also buried there. The church presently on the site was built in the fifteenth and sixteenth

centuries. Its restoration was supervised by A. V. Stoletov and I. A. Stoletov.

72. Cathedral of the Assumption of the Princess' Convent. Interior of the central apse

In 1648, on a commission of Patriarch Iosif, a team of the sovereign's painters from Moscow supervised by the master painter Mark Matveyev painted the interior of the Cathedral of the Assumption. They made each composition on the walls and the vaults solemn and captivating. The cheerful frescoes would seem to be out of place in a monastic cathedral but such was the trend of mid-seventeenth-century art.

73

73. *Prince Vsevolod III the Big Nest.* Detail of the fresco on a pillar in the Cathedral of the Assumption of the Princess' Convent. 1648

Yuri Dolgoruky's son from his second marriage to the Byzantine princess of the Comnenus dynasty, Vsevolod was nicknamed Big Nest on account of his large family. He spent several years at the court of Manuel Comnenus in Constantinople and was said to be an adher-

ent of Byzantine culture. In his reign the principality of Vladimir was recognized as the strongest in Rus and he himself was reverentially addressed as "lord", and "Vsevolod the Great".

74. *Prince Alexander Nevsky.* Detail of the fresco on a pillar in the Cathedral of the Assumption of the Princess' Convent. 1648

The prince, who became famous in Russian history through his victories over the Swedes in 1240 on the Neva and over the Teutonic Knights in 1242 on Lake Chudskoye (or Peipus), is seen here as the monk Alexei. The grandchild of "Vsevolod the Great" died suddenly in 1263 in a monastery on the Volga where he had lived as a monk on his return from his fourth journey to the Great Khan. His remains later were taken to the Monastery of Nativity in Vladimir, and in the eighteenth century Peter the Great ordered to transfer them to St. Petersburg. Before the eighteenth century Prince Alexander Nevsky was always depicted in the icons as a monk. The first icons showing him as a warrior appeared in the eighteenth century.

75. *Prince Constantine the Wise.* Detail of the fresco on a pillar in the Cathedral of the Assumption of the Princess' Convent. 1648

The elder son of Vsevolod III was the Grand Prince of Vladimir in 1216—18. His passion for reading books earned him the nickname of "Wise". He spoke several languages, he set up schools in Vladimir and Yaroslavl and had a library which contained more than a thousand books in Greek alone. "Learned men" who translated and copied books and wrote chronicles were held in high esteem at his court. The prince also was fond of painting and he commissioned icons that struck his contemporaries with their solemn compositions. He built a number of churches in Vladimir, Rostov, Yaroslavl, Ustiug and

other towns around the principality. The first church of stone for common folk was built on his orders in just four months in Vladimir's Market Place in the summer of 1218.

76. *Jacob, Isaac and Abraham in Heaven.* Detail of the fresco in the Cathedral of the Assumption of the Princess' Convent. 1648

The figures of Jacob, Abraham and Isaac in the seventeenth-century fresco are substantially different from murals of the same name in the twelfth-century Cathedral of St. Demetrius and in the fifteenth-century Cathedral of the Assumption in that they demonstrate a more sophisticated manner of painting and an obvious attempt at genre painting, characteristic of the times. The

77

exquisitely broken lines and the dispro-
portionately elongated bodies characteristic of this fresco became models in
the eighteenth to twentieth centuries
for the painters of Mstiora, Kholui and
Palekh.

77. *The Unrighteous.* Detail of *The Last
Judgement* fresco in the Cathedral of
the Assumption of the Princess' Convent.
1648

Among the sinners doomed for eternal
torments the painters included some
foreigners — Lutherans and Mohammed-
ans in characteristic West European
and Turkish costumes.

78. *Prince Andrei Bogoliubsky.* Detail
of the fresco on a pillar in the Cathedral of the Assumption of the Princess' Convent. 1648

Of interest are the images of the grand
princes of Vladimir painted on the cathedral's pillars. They are portrayed full-
length wearing sumptuously patterned

79

cloaks lined with furs and holding crosses as symbols of their devotion to Christianity and swords as symbols of power. Moscow tsars considered themselves successors to the grand princes of Vladimir. Images of the princes of Vladimir later were included in the mu-

rals of the Archangel Michael Cathedral, the last resting place of the ruling princes and tsars in the Moscow Kremlin.

79. Vladimir. View of the old part of the city

Bogoliubovo

The Church of
the Intercession-on-the-Nerl

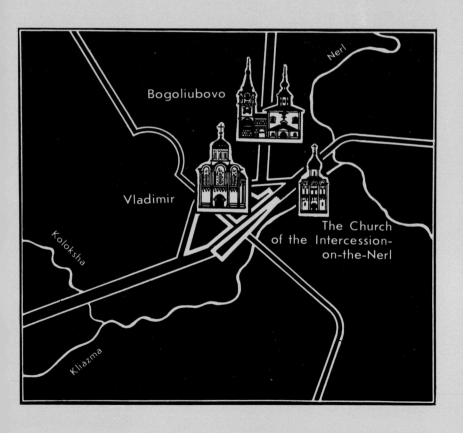

Bogoliubovo

Nerl

Vladimir

Koloksha

Kliazma

The Church
of the Intercession-
on-the-Nerl

The village of Bogoliubovo (once known as the town of Bo-goliubov) is famed in the history of the Russian people for the mark it left on twelfth-century Russian culture. It lies picturesquely on high hills which offer a fine view of the Kliazma water-meadow, the river's tight loops, the forests on its bank and the Church of the Intercession-on-the-Nerl gleaming white in the distance. Today's motorway leading to Bogoliubovo from Vladimir follows nearly the same old road bed of ancient times.

The old landmarks still standing in Bogoliubovo take us back to the eventful and turbulent beginning of Andrei Bogoliubsky's reign when, between 1158 and 1165, Vladimir, the new capital of the Suzdal land, was expanding and beautiful structures were being built in it. Since those times the course of the Kliazma has shifted to the south away from the Bogoliubovo hill. In old times the river flowed directly below the hill and what is left of it now is a marshy lake that used to be called Old Kliazma. The bank of the river was fifteen metres high and from it opened a view of the place where the Kliazma was joined by the placid and clear river Nerl flowing from the fertile heart of the Suzdal land. There are actually two Nerls, one flowing into the Kliazma, the other into the Volga, and their upper reaches are only a small distance apart. They formed an important water route for North-Eastern Rus crossing obliquely the vast and rich land. The old cities of Rostov and Suzdal were the seats of old clans of boyars with their own parochial interests who owned lands all over the Zalessky Krai up to the Moskva river. The moving of the capital to Vladimir, a young town of simple folk, struck a heavy blow to boyars' independence and threatened their political dominance. Success in the struggle they were putting on depended largely on getting possession of the Nerl waterway leading to the Kliazma. And it was at the confluence of the Nerl and the Kliazma that Prince Andrei built his fortress and opulent residence, the town of Bogoliubov.

Like in Vladimir, the choice of the site for the construction of the fortress was determined by the terrain. Extending from the north there was a deep ravine forming a cove in the Kliazma marking the town's western boundary. Its plateau which ended in steep river banks in the east and the north was not protected by any natural obstacles, and the builders had to dig a moat there in addition to earthen ramparts girdling the entire place. Although totally obliterated in the north-eastern part, the earthen ramparts and the moat still run in well-preserved condition along the western side above the ravine. The ramparts are intersected by a motorway, and to the left are the sloping hills covered with centuries-old elms. On the right side, on the ridge of the ramparts, there is a white monastery fencing. The motorway enters the former town at the same point where the road in the twelfth century did, when there was a roadway tower in the gap between the ramparts.

Legend has it that Prince Andrei built his town of stone. The chronicler's account was confirmed after the 1934—54 excavations on the southern slope of the hill yielded remains of excellent masonry, hewn white-stone foundations of a wall or a tower. Found on the ridge of the western ramparts was a powerful pedestal for a wall made of cobbles held together by white lime. Bogoliubov was the last in the series of fortresses on the Kliazma's left bank: Vladimir, the Monastery of St. Constantine and St. Helen, and the fortress above the Sungir Gully. Like these fortresses, the town of Bogoliubov was built on the site of a pre-Russian ninth — tenth-century rural settlement.

The construction of the fortress, a bold and drastic move on the part of the prince to get control of the junction of the rivers Nerl and Kliazma, must have greatly vexed the die-hard boyars. It is for this reason that the construction of the fortress had about it an aura of miracles apparently originated by the priests devoted to the prince. One legend has it that when Andrei was travelling from the south bringing with him to Rostov the "miracle-working" icon of the Virgin, the horses bearing the precious icon stopped where Bogoliubov was to be and could not be induced to take another step. In another legend as Andrei slept in his tent, the Virgin appeared to him in a vision, interceding for him with Christ and bestowing upon him her protection. This legend is commemorated in an icon which Andrei commissioned and which is now in the Vladimir museum. Unfortunately the icon has come down to us in a very poor state, but the surviving fragments still reflect something of the original expressiveness comparable with that of the famous Vladimir Virgin. Hence the icon got the name of the Bogoliubov Virgin and prompted the prince to give his new town the name of Bogoliubov (loved by God). He also took the name of Bogoliubsky.

The southern part of the town is taken up by the Bogoliubov Monastery founded in the eighteenth century in the abandoned princely palace. In order to attract more pilgrims, the monastery made the most of the legends about the icon of the Bogoliubov Virgin and the story of Prince Andrei's murder. He was made a saint in 1702. That, of course, earned the monastery money enough to engage in a vast construction. The white fence of the monastery along the motorway apparently follows the line of the old wall that used to surround the palace. The northern part was apparently where the palace servants and artisans lived. Rising over the Holy Gate of the monastery is a huge bell-tower built in 1841 with a splendid archway and a church. Looming right behind the bell-tower is the mass of the monastery cathedral built in a formal Byzantine-Russian style in 1866. Both enormous structures are in glaring disproportion with the size of the hill and the remains of the princely palace of the twelfth century.

Not much remains of the palace ensemble. After Andrei's death Bogoliubov apparently stopped commanding the attention of the princes of Vladimir. First it was gutted by Prince Gleb of Riazan; later the hurricane of the Mongol-Tartar invasion razed its fortress walls. The palace buildings, evidently, were ravaged, too, and their stones removed to be used in other monastery buildings. Standing along the southern part of the monastery wall is the Church of the Annunciation (1683) which was later greatly disfigured through alterations in the structure carried out in 1804. Its site, it is beleived, was taken by the Church of St. Leonty supposedly built by Andrei Bogoliubsky. Next to it there is a seventeenth-century chapel, "Holy Canopy", standing on the remains of one of the most intriguing structures of the seventeenth-century citadel.

There is a description of the ancient Cathedral of the Nativity of the Virgin that was still standing in the late seventeenth century. The local monastery chronicler, Father Superior Aristarchus, tells how the cathedral met its end. The then father superior of the Bogoliubov Monastery, a somewhat ignorant man, Hyppolitus, wishing to "see more light" inside the cathedral, ordered that enormous windows be made in its walls. Unable to withstand the operation the cathedral collapsed in 1722. Luckily, part of its northern wall survived, propped up by its passageway leading to the staircase tower. They have been preserved as the place where Prince Andrei was assasinated. The rubble of the collapsed cathedral was removed and the existing church was built on what remained of its walls in 1751.

It is not hard to pick out the old remaining parts on the church's western façade for their bands of blind arcading and slit windows, the hallmarks of the Vladimir builders of that period. The western wall of the present-day church is decorated with lion masks of carved stone from the old cathedral.

In the reign of Andrei Bogoliubsky, the Bogoliubov citadel was second only to Vladimir in political importance. The prince's residence was visited by envoys from neighbouring and foreign lands. It is there that the matters of war and peace and fortunes of the Vladimir lands and Rus as a whole were decided.

Nikolai Voronin

Bogoliubovo

81. Bogoliubovo. Complex of 12th — 19th-century structures

82. Bogoliubovo. Cathedral of the Nativity of the Virgin (1751) and fragments of the white-stone structures (1158—65). View from the western side

Although it came under repeated sieges over the twelfth and thirteenth centuries, was captured, gutted and burned, Andrei Bogoliubsky's fortress stood for quite a long time. The first half of the eighteenth century, however, proved to be most ruinous to the old structure. In 1722 the then father superior of the Bogoliubov Monastery

wishing to "let more light" into the cathedral, ordered its narrow windows widened. The structure could not withstand the operation and soon collapsed. The church standing on its site now was built in 1751. The tent-roofed belltower was added in the seventeenth century to the white-stone tower of the mid-twelfth century.

83

83. Icon: *The Bogoliubov Virgin.*
Mid-12th century. Tempera on wood. The
Vladimir-Suzdal Museum-Preserve of
History, Architecture and Art

The icon was painted in the 1150s on
Andrei Bogoliubsky's command to commemorate the "appearance" of the
Virgin to him in a vision when he slept.
Its creator was an outstanding painter
who succeeded in painting an image
that compared for its beauty and expressiveness with the best works of the
Byzantine school and even with the
famous icon of the Virgin of Vladimir.
Unfortunately the splendid icon has come
down to us in a very poor shape. The
surviving fragments have recently been
skilfully restored.

84. Bogoliubovo. 1158—65. The Staircase Tower of Andrei Bogoliubsky's
white-stone palace. Western façade

The palace was an unusually ornate
structure which amazed those who saw
it. Its walls of carefully hewn and
lined up stone slabs were decorated
not only with striking bands of blind
arcading, semi-colonnettes, niches and
carved reliefs, but also were lavishly
gilded and brightly painted. The white
colour of the walls and the glitter of
its gilded parts lent the fancy building
a look of something supernatural.

85

85. *Lion.* Relief on the western wall of the Cathedral of the Nativity of the Virgin in Bogoliubovo. 12th century

The builders of the new Cathedral of the Nativity (1751) put a massive lion mask in the pediment of the central window of the western wall. There is a theory that the painstakingly carved relief was one of the heads of the semi-colonnettes flanking the portal on the western wall of the original cathedral.

86. Female mask. Relief from the Cathedral of the Nativity of the Virgin in Bogoliubovo. 12th century. The Vladimir-Suzdal Museum-Preserve of History, Architecture and Art

The female masks that once adorned the walls of the court cathedral in Bogoliubovo were most probably symbols of the Virgin Mary. They are remarkable for the skilful carving and poetic treatment of a young woman's face.

87. Female mask. Relief from the Cathedral of the Nativity of the Virgin. 12th century. The Vladimir-Suzdal Museum-Preserve of History, Architecture and Art

Bogoliubovo female masks are remarkable for their exquisite forms. Even in fragments they produce one indelible impression: the cold stone seems to have come alive under the sculptor's

86

87

chisel. The female masks from Bogoliubovo can be ranked for their skilful execution not only with Russian sculptural masterpieces of the twelfth and thirteenth centuries but also with all European medieval art.

88

88. A triple-arched window and the band of blind arcading of Andrei Bogoliubsky's palace
The wall decorations of the Bogoliubovo palace have many features in common with those of Romanesque architecture in Germany, especially with the old structures in the area between the Elbe and the Rhine. According to chronicles, teams of masons employed by Prince Andrei included those sent by Frederick I of Germany. Researchers say that the castle at Wartburg has windows that resemble those of the Bogoluibovo palace.

89. Bogoliubovo. 1158—65. The Staircase Tower. Interior

The Staircase Tower is round inside, rather than square as one may surmise from its outward appearance. The winding staircase of white stone is dimly lit by four slit windows. The walls, carefully constructed from thick whitestone slabs look sombre and impenetrable.

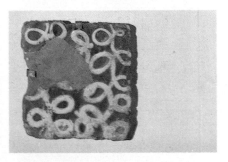

90 — 95

90—95. Majolica tiles of the floor in the Cathedral of the Nativity of the Virgin in Bogoliubovo. 1158—65

Archaeologists have found only some of the fragments of the decorations of Andrei Bogoliubsky's magnificent cathedral. Its floor was covered with sheets of copper and the floor of the prince's choir-gallery was made of majolica tiles of yellow, olive-green, brown, light and dark green colours. Some of the tiles had birds, beasts and intricate patterns painted on them.

96. Prince Andrei Bogoliubsky (1111—1174). The effigy reconstructed by Mikhail Gerasimov

The Soviet anthropologist Mikhail Gerasimov used the prince's scull to reconstruct the facial imprint of this founder of the Vladimir Principality. The son of Yuri Dolgoruky and a Polovtsi princess, Prince Andrei was an indomitable warrior, a sagacious politician and an author. Thanks to his efforts, over the period of 1157—74 the outlying area of Kievan Rus turned into a strong principality which could be ranked not only with Kiev and Novgorod, but rivalled Constantinople itself, the capital of all Europe. In a chronicler's description, Prince Andrei "wasn't big in stature, but broad and rather strong. The hair was black and curly, the forehead was large, the eyes were large and clear. He lived 63 years."

The world-famous Church of the Intercession-on-the-Nerl stands amid a water-meadow a kilometre and a half outside Bogoliubovo. As you walk towards it along the path that winds through the meadow, you see it growing before your eyes and you become fascinated by its perfectly proportioned shapes, its tall and narrow windows, portals and other smaller details. The church stands on a green hill, and its reflection is seen in a small lake formed by the Kliazma with gold and white water-lilies floating on it. It is a sight of graceful beauty and poetry. During spring floods the water rises up to the base of the church, and on occasion ice-floes knock against it.

The ravages of eight centuries have left their mark on this solitary church, several major portions of which have been irretrievably lost. In 1784, for example, the father superior of the Bogoliubov Monastery was going to dismantle the church and to use the stone to build a new belfry for the monastery. He even got the permission from the bishopric authorities. Demolition work was started but it stopped soon to never resume again because the workmen asked for higher pay which the father superior refused. The church was saved.

In 1803 its original helmet-shaped dome was replaced by the present onion-shaped cupola. A brickwork gate with a belfry on its top (the belfry was dismantled later) was built north of the church in the mid-nineteenth century. First excavations on the site were undertaken during that period with the purpose of helping the restoration of the Monastery of the Nativity in Vladimir. In 1877 the clerical authorities decided to make some repairs on the building. The damaged carved-stone details were taken down and replaced by stuccowork. The church was girdled with ugly iron bracings and given the present spherical roof above the *zakomaras* (the semi-circular upper sections of the outer walls) which concealed the rectangular pedestal and the bottom of the drum. But despite the ill-conceived repairs, the church still commands the awe and admiration of its viewers for its unusual harmony and splendour.

The construction of the church was an amazing engineering feat. It seems that Prince Andrei himself chose the location for it. The place was notorious for spring floods which rose three or more metres high, but this did not deter the builders. From its completion in 1165 to this day their creation has not been harmed by the foamy waters that lap its base each spring.

Despite the difficulties of construction, the effort was worthwhile. The church was built at the estuary of the river Nerl because it was the gateway of the Suzdal lands, leading to the Kliazma, the Oka and the Volga. Ships on the way from Suzdal and Rostov and ships carrying ambassadors and merchants from the East passed the church of the Intercession. This graceful church, the white-stone princely citadel and the sumptuous structures of the capital city of Vladimir were clearly intended to impress visitors with the might and power of the Vladimir Principality.

Legend has it that Prince Andrei built this church to celebrate his victory over the Volga Bulgars in 1164, and the stone for it was brought by the defeated people as a tribute. It was also built to commemorate Andrei's son, Iziaslav, who was killed during the campaign. As an expression of gratitude to the Blessed Virgin for her "special protection" of those who ruled the Vladimir lands, Andrei named his new church in honour of the Intercession of the Virgin and, together with the clergy of Vladimir, he proclaimed a new church holiday — the Feast of the Intercession — without seeking consent either from the Metropolitan of Kiev or the Patriarch of Constantinople. The Church of the Intercession-on-the-Nerl is the crowning achievement of the twelfth-century Vladimir architects.

Nikolai Voronin

The Church of the Intercession-on-the-Nerl

97. Church of the Intercession-on-the-Nerl. 1165. View from the north-western side

The white-stone church stands at the point where the Nerl joins the Kliazma one kilometre and a half off Bogoliubovo. Andrei Bogoliubsky built it in honour of the intercession of the Virgin. All who journeyed up the river towards the fortress in Bogoliubovo passed this graceful church.

98

98. *King David*. Relief on the northern façade of the Church of the Intercession-on-the-Nerl. 1165

The figure of King David playing his psaltery appears on three walls of the church. Birds and lions all listen to his music bewitched. Below, on the sides of the tall windows, are the figures of lions on guard, and above the windows are female masks.

99. Church of the Intercession-on-the-Nerl. 1165. View from the north-western side

The church does not look like it did originally: the artificial mound it stands on is no longer paved with stone slabs; the open gallery that surrounded the structure on three sides is no longer there; the shape of its dome has been altered. Even so the church is a perfect piece of architecture. The slim tetrahedron of the church building clearly divided into three parts on each side blends exquisitely with the surrounding landscape.

100. *Lion on Guard.* Relief on the central part of the western façade of the Church of the Intercession-on-the-Nerl. 1165

The figures of lions placed on the central sections of the church were intended as protectors of the building against evil forces. But they are also a continuation of the relief composition on the central *zakomara* of the church where King David is depicted surrounded by beasts and playing his psaltery.

101. Church of the Intercession-on-the-Nerl. 1165. Façade

The band of blind arcading is remarkable for its airiness and exquisite forms. The capitals of the colonnettes are adorned with rich carving. The corbels of the colonnettes are shaped as female heads and animals.

102

103

102. *Lions.* Detail of the relief on the western wall of the choir-gallery in the Church of the Intercession-on-the-Nerl. 1165

Inside the church there are carved stone slabs with twenty pairs of lions lying down one opposite the other. The postures of the beasts and the expressions they bear are rather diverse. Some of the lions grin smugly; others bare their teeth maliciously; still others have opened their mouths, apparently overwhelmed with great fear of some formidable force.

103. *Lion.* Corbel of the blind arcading of the Church of the Intercession-on-the-Nerl. 1165

Some corbels of the blind arcading embody forces of Good while others embody forces of Evil. Their function was to chase away from the church everything that was wicked and malicious.

104. Female mask. Relief on the central part of the western façade of the Church of the Intercession-on-the-Nerl. 1165

Some of the female masks decorating the church are round faces with wide-open eyes; others are elongated with eyes either looking down or completely closed.

105. *Leopard.* Relief from the choir-gallery of the Church of the Inter-cession-on-the-Nerl. 1165. The Vladimir-Suzdal Museum-Preserve of History, Architecture and Art

The leopard was obviously a princely symbol. Similar leopards were usually carved by Russian artists on reliefs showing the shield of St. George.

106

106. *Griffin Clawing a Doe.* Detail of
the relief on the northern façade of the
Church of the Intercession-on-the-Nerl.
1165

A griffin clawing a doe could stand
either for Good or for Evil. The griffin
was intended to intimidate enemies,
and was a symbol to induce reverence
before the powerful Vladimir prince.

107. Church of the Intercession-on-the-Nerl reflected in the lake

The majestic structure is reflected in the calm waters of the small lake formed by the Kliazma.

ВЛАДИМИР
ПАМЯТНИКИ АРХИТЕКТУРЫ

Альбом (на английском языке)
Издательство „Аврора". Ленинград. 1988
Изд. № 3170. (2-50)
Типография ВО «Внешторгиздат», Москва
Printed and bound in the USSR